CW00919318

Simon Armitage
Flit

First published in 2018
by Yorkshire Sculpture Park
West Bretton, Wakefield, WF4 4LG

ISBN 978-1-908432-35-3

Publication design & production
Sarah Coulson

Print
Graphicom, Italy

Contents

Flit

Introduction

In 2017, disillusioned by the domestic cultural scene and in search of a more depersonalised aesthetic, the poet Simon Armitage relocated to the small mid-European state of Ysp, and more particularly to its eponymous capital city. With no local contacts and only an out-dated pocket dictionary to hand, Armitage rented a small apartment in a former leprosy hospital and spent a year exploring Ysp's medieval backstreets, latter-day shopping malls, housing districts, redeveloped docks and rural hinterlands. As a stranger in a foreign country and with time on his hands, he made frequent use of Ysp's social amenities and public spaces, including its parks, gardens and museums. The poet was also briefly (and unsuccessfully) employed as a night-watchman by a company providing security services for local galleries.

The poems that emerged from this self-imposed exile or 'retreat' represent a humbling and occasionally confusing period in Armitage's life. They also form something of an alternative guidebook, describing Ysp through the eyes of an outsider, blind to familiar landmarks and official attractions.

A handful of the pieces included here are 'translations' from Ysp's most famous poet, HK. Known only by his initials, HK was most likely a Danish immigrant who arrived in Ysp in the 1890's, probably on a sea-barge or trading ship. Over the course of three or four decades he scribbled upwards of two thousand poems in the margins and end-papers of books in Ysp's National Library, some of which are still being discovered today. Written in a combination of Danish, colloquial Yspish and pigin Latin, all translations of his work are at best approximations. The stone headstone inscribed 'HK' in the central cemetery was erected in 1963; the then mayor claimed it was to honour the poet's reputation though most interpreted the gesture as a cynical ploy to attract tourists. Either way, the 'resting place' is now Ysp's fourth most visited site, even if the absence of any records relating to HK's existence suggests he died penniless and was buried as a pauper in an unmarked grave. A published undergraduate bibliography by the poet Katerina Brac, herself something of an enigma, remains the most reliable and convincing reference work on HK's poetry to this day, though it is sadly out of print.

Aubade

Those blurred indigo hours
    at the thin end of night,
        the length of the fluted spire

afloat in the violet lake,
    a purple fox on the hillock
        waiting to catch fire.

HK

Small Hours

They close the station at one a.m., the last train
being the so-called Graveyard Express,
a sleeper service with curtained windows
which pulls out noiselessly, slinking into the east.

Seen through the padlocked iron gates
the one light in the concourse spills from the shrine
of a vending machine stocked with the shiny saints
of chocolate bars and fizzy drinks, which tonight,

for reasons unknown, suddenly spews its profit
of grain-coloured coins into the empty hall.
From its roost in the rafters, a one-legged pigeon
floats down to sample the cruel feast.

The Sommelier

One evening I'd mistaken the golden glow of the Visitors'
Centre in the woods for a public bar and walked in on a private
wine-tasting event. 'Just take a seat,' said the host, assuming I
was one of his clientele and pouring me glass of chilled French
Viognier. Over the next couple of hours he talked us through
the noble art of wine-tasting and its associated techniques:
how to tip the glass towards the light and look for the 'halo'
or 'horizon' of transparency around the circumference of the
liquid; how to swirl and sniff; how to let a wine linger on the
palate to asses its 'length', and so on and so forth. 'OK to
swallow?' asked the woman in a royal-blue trouser suit sitting
in front of me, noticing the spittoon in the middle of the table.
'Why not, you've paid for it!' said the host, uncorking a near-
transparent Gavi di Gavi and moving through the room with
the bottle in one hand and a cute little towel over his free arm.
All evening he encouraged us to trust to our instincts as we
described each wine according to its aromas and flavours, and
by the time we got to the Chilean Pinos Gris I'd built up enough
confidence to throw out a few suggestions. 'Roses,' I said.
'Good,' he replied. 'Lime, potato,' I ventured after draining a
glass of off-dry German Riesling. 'Excellent,' he said. There
was a ten minute 'comfort break' before we embarked on the
reds, by which time I'd really got into the swing of it. 'Plums.
Tobacco. Chocolate,' I proposed after downing a mid-price
Argentinian Malbec. 'Very good,' said our host. A few glasses
later, after a ripe and well-balanced Zinfandel and a somewhat
indistinct Pinot Noir, I blurted out, 'Rhododendron.' 'OK'
he said, a little warily. 'Bovril. Cement. Old man's slipper,' I
shouted. 'You've tasted an old man's slipper?' he came back.
'I have now,' I said, waving a glass of Chianti Classico in his
direction. The room exploded with laughter, after which there

was no stopping me. Someone had to get the party started, and anyway, who did he think he was – the pope or something? – passing amongst us with the blood of Christ? Other people were joining in now, barking out wild and absurd comments, some of them unsanitary or sexuality explicit, and as the hilarity and barracking grew louder the defeated host eventually slipped his arms through the sleeves of his tailored linen jacket, tucked his personalised corkscrew in his breast pocket, stuffed the sheaf of tasting notes into his holdall and exited the room. After which it was just a free-for-all, everyone dispensing with ritual and formality, popping open bottle after bottle and glugging everything and anything straight from the neck, happily oblivious to issues of provenance and domain.

Although Ysp wines have no international reputation to speak of, the country claims a viticulture dating back to the medieval monasteries of the twelfth century, and climate change combined with developments in frost-resistant propagation have accounted for a significant increase in yield over recent decades. I was surprised how much knowledge I'd absorbed that night, and also how quickly I managed to scan the label of a 2015 local red before the bottle crashed against the bridge of my nose, a powerful, full-bodied Grenache/Shiraz blend from one of the newer 'boutique' wineries to the south. Staggering home in the moonlight I'd nipped into the alley behind the loading bay for a pee, and that's when he got me. 'How did that strike you?' he said, blotting a few splashes from his tailored linen jacket with a silk handkerchief. 'I'm getting liquorice, plasma, formaldehyde,' I had time to say, before my knees buckled and unconsciousness pulled its heavy canvas bag over my head.

Art and Craft

This boathouse and boat deep in the forest
were built by God. As a young man
he'd come here most days with a packed lunch
and his grandfather's carpentry tools

but moved on to increasingly complex jobs –
volcanoes, armadillos, the Great Barrier Reef –
and never came back to carve the date-plaque
or even put water in the creek.

A million million years later he's sitting
in purple robes eating his banquet-for-one
when under the last slice of Kobe beef
there they are – the stranded cedar dinghy

and open-sided shed with its shingle roof –
painted in simple Willow Pattern
on the pearlware plate. And he weeps
for the sharp steel chisels in their velvet socks,

for the spirit level's clear unblinking eye
and the hand-cranked drill, for the devout labour
of working with timber and grain.
Somewhere past and future it begins to rain.

The Impressionist

O famous reclining bronze woman
bolted to your concrete mattress
in a field full of lambs' tails and sly rooks;

tourists threw pound coins into my cup
when I mimicked your sideways mouth
and scraped-back hair and your eyes
like sheep droppings squashed on the road
and your housemaid's knees and bent spine.

Then the wind swung abruptly about
and I watched you skipping off to the woods
in your trailing skirt, dandelion clocks
exploding under your silk slippers,
leaving me metal, frozen, mute,
my eyes like half-sucked boiled sweets
spat from the mouth of a spoilt child.

Displacements

Some nights we zigzag
        down to the quay
                to gawp at the super-yachts

moored in the bay overnight,
        chrome and glass assemblies
                with permanent staff

in matching gilets and shorts,
        a cool thousand euros
                per cubic foot, unmoved

by the tipsy slosh
        of the waves.
                But the bigger dream

is the one vessel
        of rosewood and brass,
                some grand old craft

standing high in the water,
        glimpses of chandeliers,
                a wife and daughter

in matching pashminas
        descending bannistered stairs,
                verandas to all three decks

(no touching, though – you'll tarnish
      the mirrored finish,
           the high glaze).

On the dirt track
      walking home from the shore
           there's a roadside shrine

shaped as a small white church
      beaconed with candlelight.
           You can slide your arm

through the open door
      and down the aisle
           till your fingers

are four villagers, women
      huddled around the priest;
           past midnight now,

the horizon drowned
      and the last fishing boat
           still not back from the sea.

The Installation

I've picked up just enough of the native tongue
to read this report in the *Daily Post*.
A cleaner at Ysp's Museum of Modern Art
(thrown out of the matrimonial home,
it doesn't say why – 'incompatibilities' of some sort)
began spending nights in his place of work,
sneaking back after dark, disarming the sensors
then dossing down among great and priceless works.

He was found out and due to be sacked, but
crowds appeared in the evenings hoping to catch a glimpse,
staring through windows, stealing grainy snaps
of the unnamed man, some well-wishers
leaving him food, toiletries, blankets, poems and books.

Now critics have dubbed him 'the living statue',
a spectre in slippers and stripy pyjamas
drifting through half-lit galleries, cocoa in hand,
or camped on his bedroll under a bronze horse.

In the photograph, standing outside in the snow
his daughter has slipped off her woollen mitten
and touches her fingers to his through the wall of glass.

Corvus corone

Local folklore insists
the crow was an anvil once
but grew tired of the blacksmith's fist.

That its colour is pure bruise,
more purple or Prussian blue.

That only its shadow can fly.
That it shits coal, weeps tar.
That it feeds nails to its young.

That it rarely flinches, but rather
wheels slowly away
whenever sword strikes sword
in the afterlife.

That poets should steer clear,
give it a wide berth.

HK

A New Career in a New Town

David Bowie called. Before I could get into the specifics
of him being dead and this being a private, unlisted
number, he said, 'That's a foreign ring-tone, man – are
you abroad? Always had you pegged as a bit of a stop-at-
home, curled up in your Yorkshire foxhole.' I told him
I was in Ysp, flirting with communism, alienation and
Class A narcotics, and working on my experimental Ysp
trilogy. He said, 'Simon, your imagination is telling lies
in the witness box of your heart. But listen, will you write
the lyrics for my next album?' 'Why not,' I replied, and
quickly we thrashed out a plan of action. It would all be
done by electronic communication – no personal contact,
no face-to-face meetings. David *laid down some backing tracks*
and over the next year or so I worked up a suite of songs
– verse-chorus stuff, nothing too pretentious or avant-
garde. 'These are genius, man. You could have been
a poet!' he said, laughing like a cheeky cockney in the
saloon bar of a south London boozer circa 1969, his voice
like cigarette smoke blowing through a pre-loved clarinet.
'One thing I always wanted to tell you, David,' I said.
'When I was about thirteen I was really into table tennis
but had no one to play with. It was just me versus the
living room wall, on the dining room table. One night
I went down to the local youth club, where all the
roughnecks used to hang around, and made my way to
the top floor where the roughnecks were playing table
tennis, lads who'd stolen cars and thrown punches at
officers of the law. I was wearing shorts and sweatbands
in the style of my favourite Scandinavian table tennis
champion of the era whose deceptive looping serve I
hoped one day to emulate and whose life I wanted to live.

I felt like a kid goat pushed into the tiger enclosure at feeding time, but they ignored me, those roughnecks with their borstal-spot tattoos and broken teeth, just carried on playing, the small hard electron of the ball pinging back and forth across the net like the white dot in that seventies video game.' 'Pong,' said David. 'Exactly,' I said, 'Just carried on smoking and swearing and hammering the ball to and fro under the yellow thatch of the canopied light in the darkened upstairs room. And here's the thing: every time he hit a winner, the roughest of those roughnecks would sing a line from *Sound and Vision*. "Blue, blue, electric blue, that's the colour of my room," he'd croon as he crashed a forehand to the far corner of the table, or "Pale blinds drawn all day," when he flipped a cheeky backhand top-spinner past his bamboozled opponent. You probably scribbled those words on a coaster in a Berlin cocktail bar or doodled them with eye-liner pencil on a groupie's buttock, but they'd carried all the way to a dingy youth club in a disused mill under a soggy moor, into the mouth of one of those roughnecks, who's probably dead now or serving life.' David sounded pensive on the other end of the phone, perhaps even a little tearful. 'I have to go now,' he said. I could hear the technician checking his seatbelt and oxygen line for the last time, touching up his mascara, lowering his visor. Then the engines started to blast and the countdown began. I wandered down to the big Henry Moore in the park and lay on my back in the crook of its cold bronze curve, watching the skies, waiting for the crematorium of night to open its vast doors and the congregation of stars to take their places and the ceremony to begin.

Mirage

A false alarm.
    It wasn't smoke
        or heat-haze

down in the hollow,
    just a hard mirror
        of standing water

in which
    the sky blistered,
        clouds burned.

HK

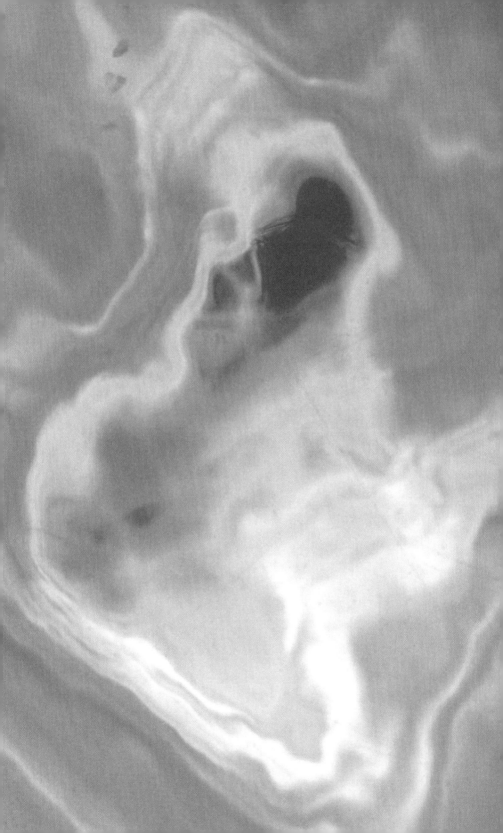

Birdlife

There's a sacred heronry now
on the lake-isle
where they hanged traitors back in the day
then left the bodies to rot.

In the glass wall of an office block
on the far bank
suited accountants roost and nest
in the mulberry trees,

each storeyed bough and branch
its own department.
Herons rise from behind desks
to get coffee or lunch,

or flounce from brain-storming sessions
and boardroom spats –
arms flapping, papers everywhere –
heading straight for the ledge.

The Manor

What a prize prick he's made of himself,
trudging a dozen furlongs across the plain

to the widowed heiress's country estate
just to be turned away at the lodge, to stare

from the wrong side of the locked gates.
The plan – admit it – was to worm his way in:

to start as a lowly gofer and drudge, then rise
from gardener to footman to keeper of hawks –

her hooded merlin steady on his wrist –
to suddenly making his way upstairs after dark,

now soaping her breasts in the roll-top bath
with its clawed gold feet, now laying a trail

of soft fruit from her pillow to his, his tongue
now coaxing the shy nasturtium flower of love.

Here he is in the dream, gilt-framed, a gent
in her late husband's best brown suit,

the loyal schnauzer gazing up at his eyes.
And here's the true him tramping the verge,

frayed collar and cuffs, brambles for hair,
the toes of his boots mouthing like grounded fish.

A pride of lions roams the walled parkland
between this dogsbody life and the next.

Cheers

Legend has it that during the *Summer of Dust*
condensation was the only drink,
and at dawn mothers were seen in the park
collecting dew from tulip petals and juniper leaves
with thimbles and razor blades.

Baptisms were outlawed that year
and only the youngest able to cry.
Radek, a former Royal Palace sentry
and last survivor from Ysp's great drought,
remembers rumours of a marble bath

in a secret room in the cathedral roof
where the archbishop was said to wallow and steam
in holy water syphoned from the font
while his people lowered buckets into the drains.
But he shrugs: 'A city must wash its face,

even when the river sleeps in the mud and bares
the crack of its arse to the skies,' he says.
And the river here is both monster and god:
curse it for its drownings and floods
and the stench it carries from farms upstream,

but to pee or even spit from the bridge
meant a week in the stocks, the stocks
now encased in glass in *Poseidon's* cellar bar
which boasts a liqueur from every nation on earth
and whose signature cocktail is *a glass of rain*.

Apple Cemetery

for James Crowden

Charles Ross,
hammered on Calvados, broke his neck.

James Grieve,
whose blossom allergy was discovered too late.

Lady Henniker,
while dozing in an orchard favoured by vipers.

Laxton Fortune,
drowned in a vat of cloudy cider.

Warners King,
slipped out of a tree.

Annie Elizabeth,
choked on a pip.

D'Arcy Spice,
shot by a rival pomologist in a duel.

Worcester Pearmain,
felled by a second helping of strudel.

The Depths

I asked the lone angler
what species of fish he was hoping to hook.

The common roach with its scarlet trim,
silver-blue armour and bloodshot eyes?
The stately carp in its golden body-stocking,
wearing its emperor's moustache?
The fidgety dace, the miserable chub,
the wingless parrot of the fancy perch?
Or maybe the nuclear sub of the pike,
nosing through slimy reeds, its undershot smile
housing a rack of talons for teeth?

But he kept a poacher's silence, statuesque
on the grass bank, his shadow
a tall thin keyhole in the river's skin,
so the pink plastic float
nodded and bobbed in his head, and the line sank
through his throat, chest, stomach, groin,
into the Ganges, Congo, Loire, Orinoco, Blue Nile.

Untitled Fragment:
'Beyond the funeral procession'

Beyond the funeral procession
        the hot-air balloon
                bears fruit.

Beyond the carnival
        the peregrine
                stoops.

HK

Émigré

I was a child of the fells and hills,
traipsed about on bald naked moors
where even a stunted hawthorn
or wooden fencepost was BIG NEWS.

So I expect marvellous things of these woods:
a venerable hornbeam hung with shoes;
a string quartet asleep and cobwebbed,
ivy wefting through the cello's nerves;

a lamppost in a clearing of pines, its glow
the underwater torchlight in a sea-cave
of luminous bugs and feathered weeds;
the great sudden galleon of a moose.

Behind me, leaves are notelets passed
from tree to tree through infinite dark,
each new poem never anything less
than a written plea for the next.

The Quick Brown Fox Jumps Over The Lazy Dog

Ever since my self-imposed exile began I've been a
regular visitor to a website called *Less Than 100 Grams*.
Dedicated to collectable ephemera of a throwaway
nature and presented in the style of an old magazine
or periodical, its twelve published issues thus far showcase
bottle tops, vintage erasers, model animals (including
a grumpy looking rhinoceros and a plastic cow), old
postage stamps, toothbrushes, guitar picks (what I would
have called plectrums), neckties, antique bookmarks,
matchbox labels, Polaroid photographs and airline
luggage tags. Issue thirteen features deformed plastic
soldiers in the shape of letters, manipulated and arranged
so as to spell out the phrase The Quick Brown Fox Jumps
Over The Lazy Dog, but the page appears only partially
constructed, leaving the impression that the creator of
Less Than 100 Grams has become disheartened at the lack
of interest in the world of miniatures, and abandoned the
whole project to go in search of a big money contract
with a multinational corporation within an expanding
economy. Or has eloped with a giant. In response, I've
found myself making my own *Less Than 100 Grams* list,
which as of this evening goes something like this: banknotes
of the world, dead leaves, earrings, beermats, fingerprints,
apostle teaspoons, butterflies of the Algarve, one night
stands, sunglasses, grass-smoke, deja-vous, Yuri Gagarin
in zero-gravity, an hour in a waiting room, echoes, boiled
sweets of the seventies, fishing stories, house keys, angel
turds, teeth, naked flames, kestrel feathers, pencil shavings,
an estimation of my own worth as expressed in terms
of metric weight, owl pellets, lipsticks, paper cuts, clouds.

The Invigilator

A quiet night in the square,
taxis parked with their side-lights on
and engines cut, drivers muttering
under a fuzzy streetlamp.
A stray dog considers an old milk carton.

Some Guevara type
comes out of the station shouting
'Smash the system',
then staggers across to the Railway Tavern.

I put the binoculars down,
take off the headphones and open the logbook;
it's vital work but written in code,
so to the untrained eye
just hieroglyphics, gobbledygook.

In his town hall office
the deputy mayor boots up his laptop
and unzips his trousers. Painstakingly
a pregnant cleaner extracts
a five pound note from the charity box
with a pair of tweezers.

Dead or Alive

The homeless, starless sky
has come to the window again
begging for crumbs and coins.

Out on the river a goose
barks at the night. A car
clears its throat in the lane.

When I turn out the lamp
the full moon stares through the glass,
five billion years old

and showing its age: pale cheeks,
its chin stippled with asteroid strikes,
dead grey lakes

under its cratered eyes.
No wait, it's a wanted poster
plastered with my face.

The Enemy's Song*

Our sons were throwbacks and runts, weaklings
who should've been drowned in a bucket at birth.
So say the fathers of those who marched to the east,
so say the fathers of Ysp.

They were bastards and freaks, embarrassing spawn
from drunken one-night stands with donkeys and pigs.
So say the mothers of those who marched to the east,
so say the mothers of Ysp.

They were droopers and dribblers and danglers,
wilting bananas and one minute wonders at most.
So say the wives of those who marched to the east,
so say the widows of Ysp

We flushed our brothers downstream like turds
then opened the windows to let out the stink.
So say the sisters of those who marched to the east,
so say the sisters of Ysp.

After the war we changed our names, doctored
their photos with crayons and razors and bleach.
So say the children of those who marched to the east,
so say the orphans of Ysp.

It's dark in the soil, dark where maggots lay eggs
in our hollow bones and our empty veins.
So say the ghosts of the men who died in the east,
so say the dead men of Ysp.

*A version of this song was allegedly chorused by the soldiers of Chall towards Ysp forces on the night before the famous battle between the two countries. If it was designed to undermine morale the gesture seriously backfired; Yspians overran their eastern enemies in a matter of hours despite inferior weaponry and an army less than a third in size, many of whom were irregulars and volunteers. Supporters of Chall's national football club have recently taken to singing the song at fixtures between the two rival teams, with a similar lack of success.

The Lodger

Sub-letting the spare room to Heidi, the struggling sculptor,
was a big mistake. Soon the beams in the kitchen
bowed under the strain of some massive marble block
and the chisel pecked away at my skull all night.

She kept herself to herself, paid her peppercorn rent
through a crack in the door, left hairs in the sink.
'This can't go on,' I said as we passed on the stairs.
She closed her eyes when she spoke: 'But he's almost done.'

A few days later the hammering stopped. Then came
the giggles, the gurgling laughter, the creaking bedsprings
even on Sunday afternoons, then the raised voices
followed by broken plates and cups, then the single shot.

Mozart's Starling

A stray brown dog walked into the gallery
under the nose of the new security guard
who was playing *Assassin's Creed* on his phone.
From here the poem might make one of two moves:
either the mutt goes padding room to room
indifferent to humanity's tortured soul,
sniffing out sweet wrappers and flapjack crumbs,
even cocking its leg against Tony Cragg's *Scribe*;
or it stands awestruck, Tony Cragg's *Skull*
reflected in the shiny buttons of its eyes, and thus
questions of animal consciousness are raised.

But reader, can I hand over the responsibility to you?
This morning I'm bored shitless by poetry;
it's a temperate Bank Holiday weekend
and I'm heading down to the garden hammock
with my iPod and a pack of craft beers from the fridge.
I'll leave a quill and parchment by the desk,
but don't dawdle: in a few minutes' time
that security guard – he's called Frank or Franz –
will turn out the master-switch and go home.

On an Overgrown Path

The alternative guidebook leads
to a partially-cleared space in the forest,
but the next page has been ripped out.

What is it I'm supposed to be looking for here?
A flint arrowhead lodged
in the trunk of an ancient oak?
The spot where Janáček sat and composed?
Is this the furthest point from the coast?

Sometimes I go upstairs
then can't remember why.
And when did these flower-arranger's hands
at the ends of my arms
become mine?

But I like this place, where a blimp crash-landed,
where ley lines cross,
where a trapdoor leads to an underground church
hewn from a seam of coal, where the sterling silver shoes
from a lost team of sacred horses
are still occasionally unearthed.

Hatches, Matches and Dispatches

A small bronze bell in the gallery roof
is somehow wired
to the city's state-of-the-art maternity suite;
forged from recycled medals

each strike signals a birth,
and visitors coo and cluck
or pull handkerchiefs out of their bags
at the kiss of metal on metal.

A double chime indicates twins,
and the day the bell pealed for quintuplets
even Karl, the hard-nosed maintenance man,
got to his feet to applaud.

Also, whenever brides and grooms
tie the knot downtown
a light snow of confetti
falls from the gallery's eaves,

and a flake plucked from the air
promises good luck. However,
a quick dimming of lights
confirms a new guest has arrived

in the city morgue, upon which
a respectful hush sets in
then dissolves. The tourists roll up,
but such jingling and sprinkling and blinking

disturbs the resident poet,
stalking the halls with his special pen,
attempting to scribble
his little ditties of life and love and death.

Espalier

I feel for that tortured apple tree,
manacled by neck and wrists
to the walled garden's red-brick wall.
Tired scarecrow of broken will,
its existence prised open from birth,
its splayed soul a forced surrender
facing the sun's inquisition all season
till it betrays its people, spills
its secrets, gives up its young.

'Don't fall for it,' said a passing fox.
'Don't blub for the crucified pain
and agonised form because really
it's sunbathing, wearing a blossom wig,
dressed in a choker and bracelets,
flaunting its double-jointed limbs
and vulgar fruits. On full moons
it slips its shackles and dances nude
with the wrinkled old oak.'

Peacetime

No one really believes those police barracks
are student dorms. Through shuttered windows
late night dog-walkers on the path through the woods
have glimpsed truncheons and braided caps
hanging on bedposts and bedroom doors,
or heard raucous gypsy-bashing songs
ricocheting among sycamores.

The constables here carry revolvers
but buy their own bullets;
low wages keep the body-count down,
though like any city
with a history worth knowing the capital boasts
gunshot holes plugged with chewing gum
at chest-height on the cathedral walls.

Overheard in the Aquarium

'He did
a poached haddock
thingummy,

which I thought
on a first date
was pretty sleazy.'

Reliquary

After the Friday market on the wharf,
dark-eyed peasant women from the east
go down on their hands and knees
with knitting needles and bird-bill pliers,
gleaning the quayside, flossing between cobbles

for dropped coins, lost keys and the like.
Whatever they winkle out that isn't currency
they sell as trinkets and charms,
spread them out on colourful headscarves and shawls
along pavements and walls.

A rough translation: 'Things that fell
from the pockets of Christ.' Meaning hairpins,
buttons, a plastic spoon, a baby's tooth,
even ring-pulls from cans of Fanta, offered
as wedding bands or knuckle dusters.

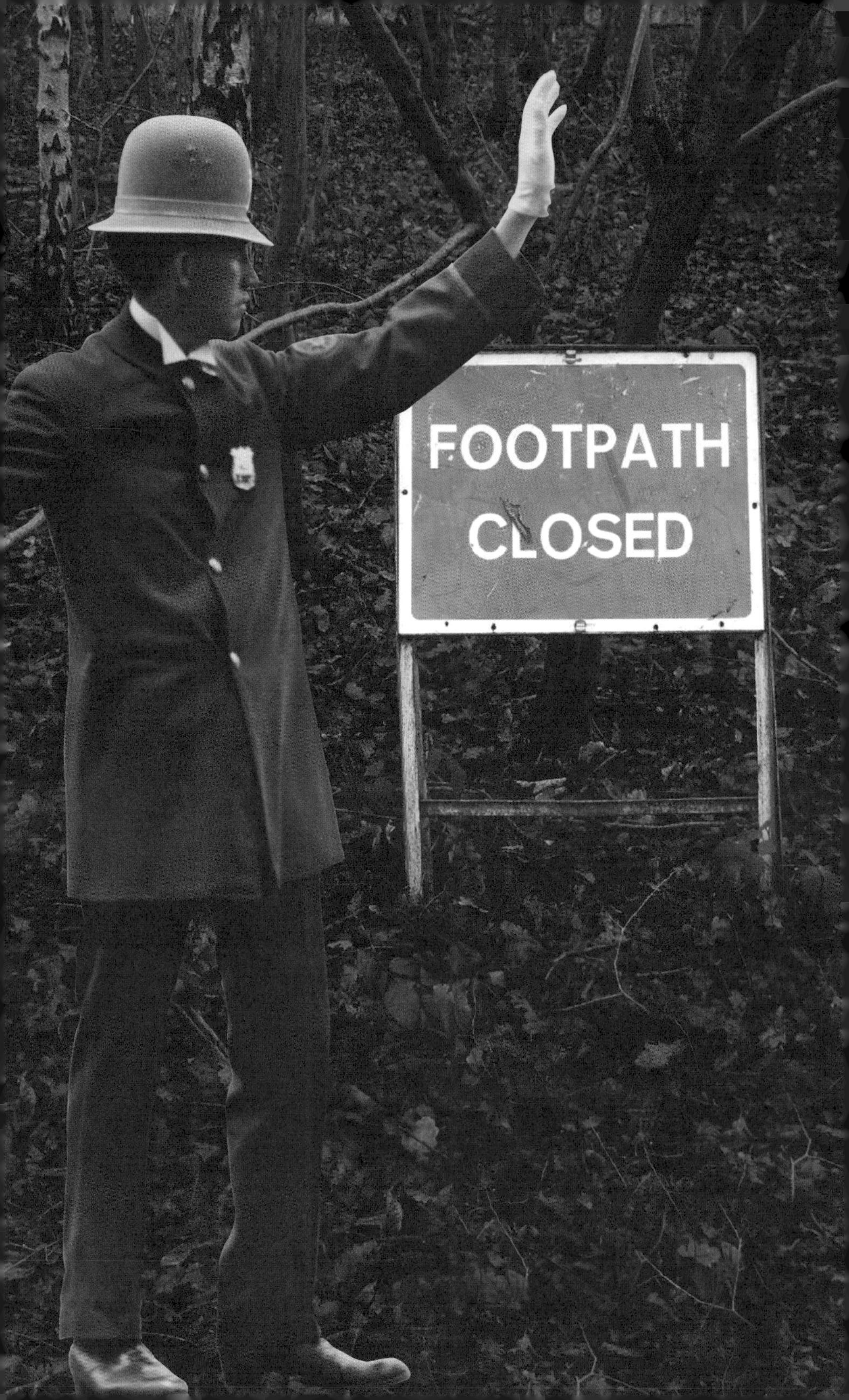
FOOTPATH
CLOSED

Self-Portrait as a Wanted Man

In every new country
he buys new shoes, shells out
the toy money of foreign currency
and wears them *there and then*,
leaves the old pair
standing in the shop
or lays them to rest

shrouded in tissue paper
in the box, or slides them
behind hotel wardrobes,
or casts them off in a lake,
or sets them down before dawn
on the steps of a church
like abandoned twins.

Then he's off down the street
giving police informers the slip,
quick feet planting false tracks,
swerving ginnel to ginnel
in fresh brakes and tyres,
tip-toeing along balcony ledges
and telephone wires.

Then

There was a queue so I joined it.
'To what end?' I asked the haberdasher in front.
'Not the foggiest, squire,' he said, 'But it's long
and it's slow. All the way to the Foundry Gates
and over the hill. It could take weeks.'

He wasn't wrong. In a month
we moved no more than a couple of yards.
But we sang songs, played Cat's Cradle,
Queenie Queenie and Blind Man's Buff,
and a caraway biscuit each was enough.

A girl with one arm piped a tune
on a flageolet made from badger's rib,
and the bloke in the calico britches
folded a hymn-sheet into the shape of a hen,
which laid an egg in his palm.

Memory, obedient friend, dutiful right-hand man,
link arms and skate with me over the frozen dam.

HK

The Dark Stairs

Each blind step
a railway sleeper
quarried from coal,
fossilised treads
marinated in tar,
charred planks
dug out of a fire.
To me they're saying
heaven or hell
it's all the same,
a minor scale
of sharps and flats,
black keys only
this way or that.

HK

Dämmerung

In later life
　　I retired from poetry,
　　　　ploughed the profits

into a family restaurant
　　in the town of Holzminden
　　　　in Lower Saxony.

It was small and traditional:
　　dark wood panelling,
　　　　deer antlers,

linen tablecloths and red candles,
　　one beer tap on the bar
　　　　and a dish of the day,

usually Bauernschnitzel.
　　Weekends were busy,
　　　　pensioners wanting

the set meal,
　　though year on year
　　　　takings were falling.

Some nights the old gang came in –
　　Jackie, Max, Lavinia,
　　　　Mike not looking at all himself.

I'd close the kitchen,
      hang up my striped apron,
            pull a bottle of peach schnapps

from the top shelf and say,
      'Mind if I join you?'
            'Are we dead yet?'

someone would ask.
      Then with a plastic toothpick
            I'd draw blood

from my little finger
      to prove we were still
            among the living.

From the veranda
      we'd breathe new scents
            from the perfume distillery

over the river,
      or watch the skyline
            for the nuclear twilight.

Untitled Fragment:
'Evening arrives, then night:'

Evening arrives,
        then night:
                an old Clydesdale

drawing a working narrowboat
        stops to nibble
                on rosehip and catmint

on the canal bank.
        The pipe-smoking bargee
                reckons here

is as good as anywhere else
        to tie up,
                and ties up.

HK

Close Season

Winter arrived this morning.
She'd flown overnight
and was tired and tetchy,
throwing her bags in the boot
and trapping her coat in the car door,
a full-length snow leopard fur
which she cheerfully told me
was *not fake*.

For a woman of such stark glamour
and minimalistic chic
she takes up a lot of space;
already she's claimed the boxroom
and several empty drawers.
She's painted the windows grey
and stands behind me, unnervingly,
if I pick up a book.

When she goes outside
to shrink-wrap the garden
and lock up the pond
I open her wardrobe,
press a cold white linen blouse
to my face, daren't even caress
the silk camisole top
stitched only by frost.

She has switched the cherry tree off.
The silvery-blue negligee
she draped on the bed
is just breath.

Visiting Katerina Brac

Not a private room
but a quiet screened-off corner of the ward
with its own lamp
and a low window facing the southern hills.
The trolley-bed
like an old sack-truck laid on its back,
the sheets
stamped and tagged, straight-jacket stiff
and bread-white,
the pillow dimpled, like somewhere a duck
had slept.
The reek from the kitchen was boiled elk.
The nurse said,
'Yes you look but photograph not allowed.'
I noted
the velvet slippers under the washstand
like dead moles,
a yellowed carton of *f6 Filterzigaretten*,
a ladybird brooch,
prescription sunglasses (four identical pairs),
the folded nightie,
the spent pistil of dried mascara stick,
and a pencil stub
which I'm ashamed to say I pocketed.
In a tall vase
a single lily was far too mortified to speak.

White Page

You're not the angel people think you are,
no holy innocent or uncorrupted child.
Twice or maybe three times a week
you're waiting down some back alley

with your little gang of bullies,
the blank canvas, the uncut stone.
'Come on, hit me why don't you, give it
your best shot,' you keep yelling

before rubbing my nose in the dirt,
grinding my hand under your heel.
Then the boots come in, and once
the splash of warm urine on my back.

The police couldn't care less, yawning,
flipping through books of suspects,
saying, 'Him? Him? How about him?',
every mugshot wearing the same empty smirk.

Last

God for a fortnight, pharaoh
till the generator blows, then what?
This week's most missed:
the shipping forecast; showing off.
Write ALIVE in the meadow
with empty blue oil drums in case
clouds can read / stars give a toss.
Two million years of shame
takes some shucking off – I still
nip behind a wall to exude.

Mandrake prospers in the cracks.
Corned beef and cling peaches again;
note to self: start growing stuff.
Along the station's oxidised tracks
every minute pulls in on time.
Ripples on the lake: ditto, ditto.
On the plus side my golf swing's
unrecognisable these days. Love is:
an afternoon in the glyptoteque
with Madam Kalashnikov.

Nocturne

        The day has counted
     its last grain of corn
into the stone jar.

        A rabbit rusts by the fence.
     Night's umbrella goes up,
moth-eaten by stars.

HK

The Dark Stones

Each third step
a railway sleeper
quarried from coal
fossilised trents
omarvantel in tar,
charcoal phalos
danyed from a fire.
The they'll sayin
heaven or hell
it's all the same
the strings and plots
of a minous scales
Under them only
all the way.

brecily dark causes   brecily dark causes
the rain crowsels top   the rain crowsels top
it will grow   stibbed on wide post.
The silver oce   the silves maching
dow amples on blorted   dow amples on blorted
is sing'd weather.   is sing weather.

No one really believed those police barracks
were student dorms.
Late night dog-walkers on the woodland path
would sometimes glimpse - through shattered windows -
polished trombones and braided caps
hanging from bed posts and bedroom doors
or held ...arus, guppy-lushing soap
bouncing between ...

The constables here carry revolvers
but buy their own ammo;
how winds keep the body-count down
but the long city with whiskey worth sending
the capital ...until bullet holes
at chest-height on the cathedral walls

No one really believed those police barracks
were student dorms.
Through shattered windows, late-night dog-walkers
on the woodland path will sometimes glimpse
polished trombones and braided caps
hanging from bed posts and bedroom doors,
or held ... carus, guppy-lushing soap
bouncing between ...

The constables here carry revolvers
but buy their own ammo;
how winds keep the body-count down
but the long city with whiskey worth sending
the city boasts bullet holes at chest-height
on the cathedral walls.

The city boasts bullet holes plugged with chewing gum
at chest-height on the cathedral walls.

Winter arrived today
She'd been there through the night
and was [illegible]

[illegible] snow lopard cat
was [illegible] told me
who [illegible]

Stick [illegible]
[illegible]

[illegible] in the window
[illegible]

[illegible]
[illegible]
is just [illegible]

She'd fallen overnight
and was first and [illegible]
[illegible] in the bed
[illegible] in the bed door
a [illegible]

For someone of such slender [illegible]
not [illegible]
[illegible] of space
[illegible] claimed
[illegible] the window
[illegible]
[illegible]

[illegible]

You don't get
to [illegible] the garden
and [illegible]
I hope [illegible]

The [illegible]   [illegible]
[illegible]   [illegible]
is just [illegible]   lisa
                                     [illegible]

Winter arrived this morning.
She'd fallen overnight
and was first and [illegible]
[illegible] in the bed
[illegible]
[illegible] to the door
[illegible] told me
[illegible] gone.

You don't get to stick
to [illegible] the garden
and [illegible] the [illegible]
[illegible] the window

For a [illegible] of such slender [illegible]
not [illegible]
[illegible] of space
[illegible] claimed
[illegible]
[illegible] the window [illegible]
[illegible]
[illegible]

to [illegible]
[illegible]
[illegible]

Credits

All photographs of Ysp by Simon Armitage except where stated.

Page 12
Collaged image: Alamy.

Page 15
Jaume Plensa *Wilsis* 2016. Courtesy the artist.

Page 19
Collaged image: Alamy.

Page 23
Collaged image: Alamy.

Page 30
Main photograph: Jonty Wilde.
Collaged image: Alamy.

Page 38
Collaged image: Alamy.

Page 41
Collaged image: Alamy.

Page 43
Tony Cragg *Secretions* 1998 (detail)
Courtesy the artist and the Deutsche Bank Collection.
Photograph: Michael Richter.

Page 47
Henry Moore *Draped Seated Woman* 1957-58 bronze
(LH 428) detail.
Reproduced by permission of The Henry Moore Foundation.
Courtesy London Borough of Tower Hamlets.

Page 48
Zak Ové *Black and Blue: The Invisble Men and the Masque of Blackness* 2016 (detail). Courtesy the artist, Vigo Gallery and Modern Forms Collection.

Page 52
Collaged image: Alamy.

Page 56
Collaged image: Alamy.

Page 64
Collaged image: Alamy.

Page 68
David Nash *Seventy-One Steps* 2010. Courtesy the artist. Collaged image: Alamy.

Page 72
Collaged image: Alamy.

Page 77
Main photograph: Jonty Wilde. Collaged image: Alamy.

Page 82
Sophie Ryder *Sitting* 2007. Courtesy the artist. Photograph: Jonty Wilde.

Acknowledgements

Acknowledgements are due to the following publications in which some of the poems first appeared:

Academy of American Poets, Australian Book Review, The Lives of Houses (Oxford Centre for Life-Writing), Oxford Review of Books, Plume, Poetry and Audience, The Poetry Archive, Sewanee Review.